Valentine's Day

BY
Cass R. Sandak

CRESTWOOD HOUSE
New York

Library of Congress Cataloging-in-Publication Data
Sandak, Cass R.
  Valentine's Day

  p.   cm.—(Holidays)
  Includes bibliographical references.
  Summary: Presents the history and customs of Valentine's Day.
  1. Saint Valentine's Day—Juvenile literature. [1. Valentine's Day.]   I. Title. II. Series: Holidays
GT4925.S26   1990   394.2'683—dc20   89-25408   CIP
ISBN 0-89686-504-5   AC

Photo Credits
Cover: Journalism Services: W.S. Nawrocki
Journalism Services: (Chris Marona) 4; (W.S. Nawrocki) 26; (M. West Kinney) 37
Culver Pictures, Inc.: 7, 8, 10, 15, 16, 17, 19, 21, 23, 24, 31, 32, 39, 40, 43, 44, 48
Berg & Associates: (Dick Wade) 29, 35

Macmillan Publishing Company
866 Third Avenue
New York, NY 10022
Collier Macmillan Canada, Inc.

Printed in the United States

First Edition

10 9 8 7 6 5 4 3 2 1

Contents

A Time to Celebrate Love

Valentine's Day is a time to celebrate love and friendship. Love and friendship are very important parts of our lives. It should not seem at all strange, therefore, that there is a holiday devoted to love and lovers, friendship and friends.

Valentine's Day is a time to tell people that we like them or love them. We can do this in a number of ways throughout the year. But on Valentine's Day we send people valentines. These are little cards or notes that say "Be My Valentine."

When we speak of love, we don't just mean between girlfriends and boyfriends. We don't just mean love between husbands and wives. We don't just mean love between mothers and fathers. There are many kinds of love:

love in families,

love between parents and children,

love between brothers and sisters,

love for cousins, aunts, uncles, and other relatives,

love for friends, schoolmates, and teachers,

and love for other people in our lives.

Love includes many different things. It means sharing good times and bad times. It may mean a feeling of warmth and security. Or it may mean comfort and forgiveness. Valentine's Day is a time when everyone who is in love or who ever has been in love wants to remember those special feelings. The three little words "I love you" hold an entire lifetime of meaning.

Valentine's Day is a traditional celebration. It is not a religious or a legal holiday. It is different from many of our holidays, since schools,

Hearts, flowers, and kisses are universal emblems of Valentine's Day.

stores, and banks remain open. After Christmas, it is one of the most popular holidays.

The things we do at Valentine's Day are very old customs. They center around the idea of love. They are also connected with the story of the Saint of Love — Saint Valentine. In fact, the proper name for the holiday is Saint Valentine's Day. But the traditions of the holiday go back in time even before Saint Valentine. Some of these traditions concern stories of ancient gods and goddesses of love.

An Ancient Roman Holiday

The story of Valentine's Day begins more than 2,000 years ago in ancient Rome. One of the Romans' most important holidays was the feast of Lupercalia. It began each year on February 15 and continued for several days. Lupercalia honored several different gods and goddesses.

The festival's name came from Lupercus, the god of herds and crops. Lupercus protected people and their flocks against wolves. He also brought them luck in having children.

Another god associated with the festival was Faunus (or Pan), the god of nature. The worship of Pan often involved drunkenness and wild parties. The Roman gods and goddesses were not always well behaved!

The day before Lupercalia was a holiday, too. February 14 was a day to honor Juno, the queen of the Roman gods and goddesses. She was also the goddess of women and marriage. This celebration of Juno's is probably why February 14 became a special time for couples and sweethearts.

Half-goat and half-man, Pan was the Greek and Roman god of
6   revelry.

CAVTO PANI.
C · MVNATIVS
QVIR · TIRO II VIR
I · D · ET C · MVN
ATIVS FRONTO
FILIVS · D · D ·

7

HG.

Roman girls and boys did not go to school together. Nor did they play together as modern children do. However, during the feast of Juno on February 14, this situation changed. On that day young Roman boys chose the names of girls from a large urn or vase. These names had been written on pieces of parchment. Then the boy and the girl whose name he picked became partners in games and dances throughout the Lupercalia festival. Sometimes the pairing lasted for a whole year. Often the two ended up falling in love and getting married.

The Romans brought the celebration of Lupercalia and the feast of Juno to the British Isles when they made Britain a province of their empire. Later, February 14 became a Christian celebration connected with Saint Valentine. The holiday took on a new meaning both in Rome and in Britain and other parts of the Roman Empire. In place of the rowdy festival of Lupercalia on February 15, February 14 came to be celebrated as the feast day of Saint Valentine.

A Saint Named Valentine

According to the Roman Catholic Church, there are eight different saints named Valentine. These different Valentines lived in widely scattered places including Africa, Spain, France, and Belgium. Two or three of them lived in or near the city of Rome. And seven of them had feast days that fell on the same day — February 14!

It seems that the most famous saint named Valentine, however, was a priest who lived in Rome around the year A.D. 270. This was dur-

Juno surrounded by some of her symbols.

ing the reign of the Emperor Claudius II. At that time, most Romans still believed in their old gods and goddesses such as Jupiter, Juno, Venus, and Mercury. Christians could not worship openly. To be a Christian and refuse to worship the gods of Rome was a crime. Many Christians were imprisoned because of their beliefs.

One story says that the emperor Claudius had forbidden young men to marry because he wanted them as recruits for the Roman army. The soldiers were to be sent to distant provinces of the empire. The emperor wanted the men to be free of wives and sweethearts. The brave priest named Valentine defied the decree. He performed secret marriage ceremonies for young couples. He continued doing this until he was arrested and placed in prison. He thus earned the respect of young couples everywhere.

The legends of Saint Valentine tell of his kindness and love for children. Even after he was put in jail for his beliefs, Saint Valentine

Valentine was imprisoned because he refused to give up his religion, but he continued to perform Christian rites in jail.

remained cheerful and kind. His friends showed their love for him. They tossed messages and small bouquets of flowers to him through the window of his cell. Many people think that may have helped start the custom of sending love letters on Valentine's Day. According to another story, the first valentine message may have come from Valentine himself.

Apparently, a jailer in Valentine's prison had a young daughter. Her name was Julia, and she was blind. The legend says that Valentine cured Julia's blindness. Despite the miracle, Valentine was sentenced to die because he refused to worship the Roman gods.

On the night before he was to be beheaded, Valentine sent a note to the young woman he had cured. He assured her that it was not her fault that he had been sentenced to death. He signed the note "From Your Valentine."

Saint Valentine's head was cut off on February 14. The beheading took place on Rome's Palatine Hill, not far from a shrine dedicated to the god Pan. Two centuries later, in A.D. 496, a pope named Gelasius I declared February 14 the feast day of Saint Valentine the martyr. (A martyr is someone who has died because of his or her religious beliefs.)

The Holiday Through the Ages

Shortly after Saint Valentine's death, the Roman Empire became Christian. The old festival season in February was kept. But the customs associated with Lupercalia were given new meanings. The pairing of young couples also continued. Now, however, it became part of the Christian celebration of Saint Valentine's Day.

Roman Catholic priests who came after Saint Valentine abolished the old Lupercalia custom of boys choosing the names of girls for games and dances. They shifted the emphasis away from what they considered a sinful pagan custom. They substituted the names of saints for the names of girls on the slips of paper. After drawing the name of a particular saint, the child studied his or her life and asked for the saint's prayers.

Gradually, the idea of Saint Valentine's Day spread from Rome to other parts of Europe. The holiday became popular in the British Isles, France, and Scandinavia.

In Italy, around the year 1000, young men and women gathered in gardens and courtyards on Saint Valentine's Day. They would stroll through the grounds singing songs, listening to music, and reciting poetry. Then for a time, celebrations of the holiday died out. The Church frowned on activities that might be considered immoral or frivolous.

By about 1400, it became the custom for young men to send their sweethearts gifts on Valentine's Day. These gifts might be flowers or birds in a cage. If the young men were rich, they gave very expensive gifts. Noblemen or princes would send their ladies gold rings, bracelets, or necklaces.

The rituals of love and courtship in the Middle Ages also found their way into the traditions and customs of Valentine's Day. A knight in the Middle Ages often wore a token as a reminder of his lady when he rode into battle or fought in a tournament. Sometimes the token was a ribbon, a piece of lace, or a handkerchief. That is why many valentine cards today are trimmed with ribbons or pieces of velvet, satin, or lace.

Lovers also wore each other's sleeves as a sign of love. Clothes in the Middle Ages were often made with sleeves that could be removed and washed separately from the main part of the shirt, jacket, or gown. Lovers could exchange sleeves the way people today exchange rings, or girls wear their boyfriends' football sweaters. The expression "to wear one's heart on one's sleeve" comes from this tradition.

When pocket watches became popular in the late 18th and 19th centuries, a new valentine custom developed. Women would embroider small love tokens the size and shape of pocket watches. Sometimes they stitched in their initials or love messages. Men would keep tokens such as these inside their watch cases.

Hundreds of years ago in England, children went from house to house on the morning of Saint Valentine's Day. This was done at almost every holiday, including Christmas, Easter, and even Halloween. On Valentine's Day, children sang and begged for pennies or other small treats.

For a brief time in England, during the mid-17th century, it was considered immoral to send valentines or exchange gifts. But when Charles II returned to the English throne in 1660, many old customs and practices came back into fashion. Luxurious items such as perfumed gloves or jeweled garters became popular Valentine's Day gifts for ladies and gentlemen wealthy enough to afford them.

In America, Valentine's Day was first celebrated by settlers from the British Isles. During the Civil War, Valentine's Day was considered the most important holiday in the United States after Christmas. Periods of war have always been special times for lovers. Most soldiers are young men who have sweethearts back home. Love letters and messages become especially important to couples who are separated. Saint Valentine's Day takes on special meaning for them.

Valentine's Day Traditions

Several interesting ideas about Valentine's Day have come down to us from the past. Spring arrives early in Europe. People long ago noticed that birds choose their mates in mid-February. When birds return in the spring from their migrations and start to build their nests, people start to think about love and marriage.

Pictures of birds often appear on Valentine's Day cards or in decorations. Because birds can fly and sing, they seem to stand for freedom and happiness. Some birds keep the same mates all their lives. They are therefore considered symbols of love and faithfulness. We call two people who are very happy together "lovebirds."

In the 14th century, people believed that birds began to mate on Saint Valentine's Day. So it seemed only natural that — like the Romans — young men and women should also choose Valentine's Day to find their own sweethearts. Over the years, Saint Valentine's Day has become a favorite date for weddings.

Other beliefs about dating and mating grew up about the holiday. In Shakespeare's *Hamlet*, the love-sick Ophelia sings:

> Good morrow! 'tis Saint Valentine's Day
> All in the morning betime,
> And I a maid at your window,
> To be your Valentine!

In Ophelia's song, Shakespeare is referring to the old saying (that was old even in his time) that the first person you see on Valentine's Day will be your valentine. No doubt the belief has led many young men and women to camp out beside their sweethearts' windows on Valentine's Day morning!

An old-fashioned Valentine celebrating some of the best feelings of the holiday: truth, friendship, sincerity, and, of course, love.

In the drawing done in 1802, Cupid leads a young couple deeper into love.

It seems logical that there should also be traditions about kissing. To be awakened by a kiss on Valentine's Day is considered very good luck. And some people believe you will see your lover's face in a dream on Valentine's Eve if you sleep with the leaves of certain plants pinned inside your pillow.

Not content with seeing their lovers' faces in dreams, some maidens went a few steps further. At midnight on Valentine's Eve they would gather in the local churchyard. They ran twelve times around the church as they scattered seeds from their aprons or baskets. They repeated the old rhyme:

> I sow hempseed, hempseed I sow,
> He that loves me best come after me now.

No doubt the girls' wishes often came true. The boys would chase the girls through the churchyard. And the girls hoped to be caught. They usually ran with their heads turned back over their shoulders. This way they could catch sight of their boyfriends.

Hearts and Flowers

Hearts

We see many signs and symbols on Valentine's Day cards and decorations for the holiday. All of them have special meanings.

The red heart is an old symbol for love. Centuries ago, people knew nothing about the way the heart pumps blood through the circulatory system. They knew that the heart beats faster when a person is excited or upset. For this reason people thought the heart was the center of our feelings. Some of this feeling remains today. When we are happy

The heart in the middle of this Valentine swings open to reveal a verse.

about something, we may say, "It does my heart good." Or when we are sad or disappointed we may say, "I'm broken-hearted." Experiences may be "heart-warming" or make us "sick at heart."

The heart is also connected with one of the ancient Roman gods, Cupid. Cupid was the son of Venus, the goddess of love. Cupid was a god of love in his own right, and his name comes from the Latin word for desire. Sometimes he is referred to as Dan Cupid. The "Dan" is a changed form of the word "Don" which means "Mister" or "Sir" in Spanish. The Greeks called this same god Eros. In paintings and statues, he is shown either as a beautiful young man or as a chubby, curly-headed young boy with wings.

In myths and legends, Cupid flew around shooting arrows into people's hearts. The arrows didn't kill them. They made people fall in love with whoever was nearby. Often Cupid shot his arrows with little thought or care. Because of this, the most unlikely people would sometimes fall in love with each other. We still use the expression, "Love is blind." It means that it is often hard to understand why two people have fallen in love. It must be because Cupid was blind when he shot his arrows!

Over the centuries, Cupid's mischief got many people into trouble, including himself. The story of Cupid's love for Psyche is one of the most popular myths to come down to us from the ancient world. Venus was jealous of a beautiful princess named Psyche. Venus's son, Cupid, made the mistake of falling in love with the girl. Venus's desire for revenge almost destroyed Cupid and Psyche. But in the end, after the trials and triumphs of love, the mortal princess became a goddess. She and Cupid went to live forever in bliss on Mount Olympus. The story shows the many sides of love: beauty, trust, mystery, disappointment, jealousy, forgiveness, patience, and reconciliation.

Another frequently used heart symbol is a pattern of interlocking circles called the "true-love knot." It stands for two hearts joined

Cupid sharpening one of his arrows

together as one. The design has been popular for hundreds of years. It has been used in jewelry, in needlework, in quilts, and in the layout of flower beds in some gardens.

Sometimes the love-knot design is joined with a capital letter "A" that may or may not be decorated with a crown. The "A" stands for the Latin phrase, "Amor vincit omnia." It means "Love conquers all."

Flowers

Flowers have been symbols of love and happiness for a long time. Today, people often send flowers as gifts. Or they use them as decorations on Valentine's Day. With their beautiful shapes and colors and scents, flowers naturally remind people of romance. When flowers are dried or pressed between the pages of a book, their messages of love can live on.

Flowers can also send more specific messages. The language of flowers developed over a period of centuries.

For instance, to some people, an iris added to a bouquet of flowers sends a message all its own. It means "Look at the other flowers and see what they say." Red tulips are a declaration of love. Yellow tulips mean "My love seems hopeless." The names of such flowers as "bleeding heart" or "love-lies-bleeding" seem to tell their own sad stories of love that is not returned. Even the leaves of plants and flowers may have special meaning. Green stands for hope. A cluster of chestnut leaves means "I hope that you will treat me fairly."

Since earliest times, roses have been prized as the most beautiful of flowers. The rose was sacred to Venus, the ancient goddess of love. Long-stemmed, red American Beauty roses have a special

This Valentine cut in the shape of a bellows was meant to fan the flames of love.

meaning for lovers. On Valentine's Day, one red rose or a dozen means "I love you."

Sometimes, however, there is a difference in meaning attached to flowers by people who live in different cultures.

There is an old English tradition about a flower called the snowdrop. People thought it was unlucky to bring one into the house before Valentine's Day. It meant none of the single daughters in the household would find a husband for a whole year!

In Denmark, however, snowdrops are considered lucky flowers on Valentine's Day. Danes often put dried and pressed snowdrops in their valentine notes and messages.

"Bachelor's buttons" are also thought to be lucky. If a man wears one on Valentine's Day, it is supposed to mean he will marry his sweetheart within a year.

The violet has a special Valentine's Day meaning. Legend has it that violets grew outside the window of the jail where Saint Valentine was imprisoned. Some stories say Valentine was able to reach out and spell messages with the flowers. In the language of flowers, violets stand for faithfulness.

That may be why the amethyst, a violet-colored stone, has become the birthstone for February. Long connected with the story of Saint Valentine, the violet-colored stone is considered lucky for lovers.

Valentine's Day Cards

Perhaps one of the oldest Valentine's Day customs is sending valentines. As early as the 14th century, people sent Valentine's Day greetings and messages to each other. The earliest paper valentine we know of is in the collection of the British Library in London. A Frenchman, the duke of Orléans, wrote the verses to his wife in 1415. He had been captured by British soldiers at the Battle of Agincourt. The duke was a prisoner in the Tower of London when he penned the message.

Over the next centuries, sending Valentine's Day notes or letters became very popular. There were even books explaining how to write valentine messages and verses. In colonial times in America, the Puritans of New England frowned on Valentine's Day celebrations as frivolous. By about 1750, however, the custom of sending valentines took hold. The first valentines in the United States were made by hand. People wrote their notes or verses on pieces of paper. Then they drew designs or pictures around the verses.

It was not until the 1800s in England that stationery companies began making valentines. At first, they were printed on single unfolded sheets of paper. Later, companies started making the stiff cards of folded paper we know today. They also started making very

Two young women blush over a 19th-century Valentine printed on an unfolded sheet of paper.

A mailman delivers cards to a lively Victorian family.

complicated valentines. Some of them were made up of seven hundred separate pieces that had to be glued and fitted together by hand. The most elaborate ones had three thousand pieces! These cards cost a lot of money.

Until the mid-1800s, companies in England dominated the Valentine's Day card industry. They shipped their cards to be sold all over the world. About 1847, however, an American businesswoman named Esther Howland came on the scene. In her home in Worcester, Massachusetts, she set up a workroom to manufacture valentines. The cards were sold in her father's stationery store. She used the finest materials — embossed papers, satin backing, paper lace, and cut-out ornaments pasted down by hand. By 1849, Miss Howland's card business was a big success.

The first machine-made valentines were not introduced into the United States until 1880. These were less expensive. But they lacked the personality and individual touches of the earlier hand-made cards.

Then companies started to make many different kinds of valentines. Some were word puzzles. Acrostic verses were popular, too. In an acrostic, the first letter of the word that begins each line spells out a name or special word. Another kind of valentine had to be folded a certain way to be read. Others were painted by famous illustrators such as Kate Greenaway and Walter Crane.

Some valentines had little mirrors glued to them to reflect the faces of the people who received them. Others bore photographs of the people who sent them. These were special valentines. Cameras were new, and it took time and money to make a photograph.

Many valentines were decorated with cutout designs made from cloth or paper. Others had designs made with pinholes or were decorated with pieces of paper lace. Some valentines had parts that could be moved by pulling little tabs.

Of course, there are all kinds of valentines. They can be sweet and romantic. Or they can be silly and rely on word games or puns to get their messages across. For example, a picture of a Hawaiian hula dancer decked in island fruits might bear the message: "I *pine* for you, *apple* of my eye."

Drawing Names

The custom of choosing names started by the early Romans continued in the Middle Ages. Young men and women in England, Scotland, and France picked the names of their holiday sweethearts out of an urn on the night before Valentine's Day.

Today people still draw names or lots at Valentine's Day parties. Each guest writes his or her name on a piece of paper or a notecard. When all the names have been collected and put into a container, guests take turns being blindfolded and drawing a name. If the guest draws the name of a person of the same sex, the lot may be thrown back into the bowl and the person draws again. This process continues until everyone is paired.

The game can be a good way to get to know new people. It is wise to remember that it is only a game. No one has to fall in love with his or her partner! And it is a game that people of any age can play.

Another form of this old custom is drawing names from a valentine box. In many schools, students still put their valentine cards into brightly decorated boxes. At the end of the day, students take turns drawing out a handful of cards and delivering them to the right people. Or they appoint a Valentine's Day letter carrier to deliver all the cards from the box.

A pop-up Valentine from the turn of the century.

Parties for a Special Day

Since the Middle Ages, the night before Saint Valentine's Day has been a favorite time for parties and balls. Today parties and dances are often held in schools on Valentine's Day.

Decorations featuring various Valentine's Day symbols get people in the proper mood. So do other customs of the day. Some people, for instance, choose special themes for their parties. And by tradition, people still play games that involve choosing partners. Divination games are especially popular. They are games that pretend to see into the future. Sometimes they may give a glimpse of one's future sweetheart.

One form of divination involves throwing a handful of seeds into a bowl or pan of water and asking "Who will be my sweetheart?" The answer is revealed in the pattern that the seeds form on the surface of the water. They may form the initial of a name.

Yet another kind of divination can be done using three bowls of water. One should be empty, one full, and one half full. A blindfolded player reaches out to stick his or her hand into one of the bowls. The bowls, of course, have been shifted around. If the player picks the full bowl, he or she will marry his or her sweetheart. If the empty bowl is selected, the player will die an old maid or bachelor. If the half-full bowl is chosen, it may mean one of many things: hardship in love, a long engagement, or marriage to a widow or divorcee.

Another popular game is "She loves me. She loves me not." A player tears off the petals of a flower one by one, repeating "She loves me" and then "She loves me not" with each petal. The answer to the mystery of whether the player is loved lies in the last petal of the

A young artist displays his latest creations—a laced Valentine and a Valentine box.

flower. (If a person doesn't like the answer, she or he can always try again with another flower!)

Today, people like to serve anything heart-shaped on Valentine's Day. They make heart-shaped cookies and sandwiches with heart-shaped cookie cutters, and gelatine salads with heart-shaped molds. People have been known to include some cherries and passion fruit!

Some foods are traditional on Valentine's Day because in earlier times it was thought certain foods and drinks could be used to put one in the mood for love. Among these items were spiced wine and eggs. Apples were also important symbols of love. Pears were sacred to Venus, the goddess of love. Figs and pomegranates were associated with ancient goddesses of love and fertility in the Mediterranean world. And cherries, plums, raisins, currants, and other fruits have also been included on many Valentine's Day tables.

Baker's clay can be used to make valentine symbols such as hearts, flowers, birds, and cupids. A cookie cutter might make them easier to fashion, but they can also be modeled by hand. When they are dried and painted, drill a hole through them. Then loop a piece of yarn or string through and tie it with a knot. The figures can be used as necklaces or tied to tree branches painted white to make a Valentine's Day tree.

Around the World Today

Valentine's Day is still observed mostly in Europe and North America. And it is usually celebrated by exchanging cards and small gifts. In fact, Americans and Canadians send more cards at Valentine's Day than at any other time of the year except Christmas.

To my best
·Love·

Dan Cupid dressed up like a royal courtier.

A drawing of a little girl presenting a bouquet to a venerable old man.

But recently, Valentine's Day has become popular in Japan. Women there have started to send their male friends or sweethearts cards or flowers. As in the western world, Japanese stores frequently use the holiday as a theme for decorating and for advertising and special sales.

In Great Britain and parts of the world settled by British people, people send cards. Children often receive gifts of candy or money. Traditional buns filled with raisins, currants, caraway seeds, or plum preserves are popular treats.

In countries that are mostly Roman Catholic, the holiday still has much of the flavor of the original feast of Saint Valentine. Churches hold special masses that include prayers that mention the saint (or saints) named Valentine. Italy, Spain, Belgium, and some other places still observe the holiday in this way. Young people often go to dances or parties with a Valentine's Day theme.

In Sicily, the Valentine's Day custom is for a young, unmarried girl to stand at her window half an hour before sunrise on the holiday. If she sees a man walk by, he or someone who looks like him will become her husband within a year, or so they say.

Popular Valentine Gifts

After Christmas, Valentine's Day is the most popular day in the year for giving and receiving gifts. In schools and homes and businesses, cards and gifts for friends and loved ones are the order of the day. Heart-shaped boxes of candy are favorite gifts for both young and old.

Grown-ups like to send valentine gifts. Your father might give your mother a fancy box of chocolates or a bouquet of flowers. Your mother might give your father a shirt or tie or cufflinks. Things that smell nice, like perfumes and colognes, are other good gift ideas. Popular Valentine's Day presents include heart-shaped pieces of jewelry, or heart-shaped boxes made from wood, china, leather- or papier-mâché. Some people would welcome glass or porcelain novelty figurines. One representing famous sweethearts — Romeo and Juliet, for example — would be especially appropriate. Books, too, make nice gifts. Valentine's Day presents should show thought and imagination.

Sometimes lovers will run long distances or bicycle many miles just so they can deliver valentine messages or gifts in person. It is possible to place a Valentine's Day message in the classified section of the local newspaper. Many papers print special pages of personal notices on Valentine's Day. And it doesn't cost very much.

A person might hire an airplane to skywrite a message. One television star had jet pilots make a heart three miles wide pierced by a six-mile-long arrow! In the past, noblemen would give their sweethearts rare birds or precious jewels. Whether they are paper or porcelain, plain or fantastic, valentine gifts say, "You are special. I love you."

Valentine's Day is one of the happiest holidays we celebrate. Each time we follow the customs of the day, we give new meanings to an old holiday. The traditions of Valentine's Day have a long history. But each time we send a valentine, the message is fresh and new. We are saying "I like you" or "I love you" in the same way that people have done for hundreds of years.

Today kids can buy ready-made cards for their friends and classmates.

Valentine's Day Trivia

The Name Valentine

The *Golden Legend*, written in the Middle Ages, is a treasury of information about the lives of the saints. It says the name "valentine" may come from either of two Latin phrases. One is *valens tiro*, which means a strong warrior. The other is *valorem tenens*, which means one persevering in holiness. Monks in the Middle Ages often made up derivations of names or words when they wanted to make a point or teach a lesson. Sometimes they had to stretch the language to do so.

Other scholars suggest that the Latin name *Valentine* (or *Valentinus*) is related to the French word *galantin*, meaning a lover, or gallant. The English words *valiant* and *gallant* are related and mean much the same thing. It seems especially appropriate that a saint named Valentine should be the special patron of lovers and sweethearts.

The Saint Valentine's Day Massacre

An ugly gangland battle that left seven men riddled with bullets was called the Saint Valentine's Day Massacre because it took place on February 14, 1929. The victims were thugs themselves, seven members of "Bugs" Moran's gang. They had been lured to a parking garage on Clark Street in Chicago. After the men were lined up against the wall, members of Al Capone's mob opened fire on them with machine guns. The actual murderers in this gangster-style execution, were never identified or brought to trial.

When Cupid sprang to life on the cover of this 1915 magazine, his target greeted him with delight.

CHICAGO SUNDAY HERALD
SUNDAY MAGAZINE

CHICAGO, ILLINOIS
FEBRUARY 14, 1915
20 PAGES
PART 3

No Quarter

M. WEST KINNEY

With Tears in Her Eyes: A German Valentine's Day Custom

To find out who her husband would be, a German girl would plant onions in clay pots on Saint Valentine's Day. On each pot, she placed a name tag. The name on the first onion to sprout would be the name of the boy she would marry.

The Valentine Contract

The standard legal contract that actors who work in London theaters sign is called a "valentine" contract. It provides that any agreement is null and void if the play is scheduled to be performed on a stage or other area that is not licensed. In addition, any play to be performed must previously have been approved by the Lord Chamberlain, a government official. The reason this kind of contract is called a "valentine" has been lost to history.

Artists never seemed to tire of drawing cupids and women: this one was called "The Dangerous Playmate."

39

PET OF MY HEART

IF I WERE STARVING I
COULD DEVOUR YOUR LOOKS;
IF I WERE DYING OF THIRST,
I COULD DRINK YOUR WORDS;
IF I WERE BURNING,
YOUR COLDNESS
WOULD FREEZE ME,
AND IF I WERE
FREEZING, YOUR SMILE
WOULD
WARM ME
BACK TO LIFE.

A Valentine's Day "Sweetheart" Deal for British Trade

The Valentine's Day Formula was a document issued on February 14, 1906, by British prime minister Arthur James Balfour. It formed part of a campaign platform in support of the Union Movement in Britain. It called for reforms in British fiscal policy including a tax on manufactured goods. A duty or tax was also to be placed on grain imported from other countries.

Valentine and Orson

"Valentine and Orson" is the name of a story in verse popular around 1400. The story tells about twin brothers who were abandoned in a forest shortly after their birth. Orson was raised by a bear and grew up to be a wild man. Valentine was a courteous and valiant knight raised in the court of King Pippin of France. When the two brothers meet, Orson is tamed by Valentine. The pair become inseparable. The two go on to rescue their mother, Bellisant, from an evil giant.

A boy in knickers woos a coy mistress with a heart and verse.

Valentines and Dracula

The famous horror movie *Dracula*, starring the Hungarian actor Bela Lugosi was released on Valentine's Day 1931! The movie was based on a vampire novel about a blood sucking Count Dracula. The book was written by Bram Stoker.

A Perfect Valentine's Heart

To make a heart that is even on both sides, fold a piece of paper in half. Then draw half a heart shape along the edge that is folded. Leaving the paper folded, use scissors to cut along the line you have drawn. When the paper is unfolded you will have a heart that is the same size and shape on each side.

Women in a 19th century factory mass produce Valentines.

The little heartbreaker on a card made in 1901

For Further Reading

Barth, Edna. *Cupid and Psyche*. New York: Clarion: The Seabury Press, 1976.

———. *Hearts, Cupids and Red Roses*. New York: The Seabury Press, 1974.

Brown, Fern G. *Valentine's Day*. New York: Frankin Watts, 1983.

Cosman, Madeleine Pelner. *Medieval Holidays and Festivals*. New York: Charles Scribner's Sons, 1981.

Sandak, Cass R., *Valentine's Day*. New York: Franklin Watts, 1980.

Sechrist, Elizabeth Hough. *Red Letter Days, A Book of Holiday Customs* (revised edition). Philadelphia: Macrae Smith Company, 1965.

Staff, Frank. *The Valentine and Its Origins*. New York: Praeger Publishers Inc., 1969.

Index